To:

_____

From:

_____

♥ Message: ♥

_____

_____

_____

THE BiBLE STORYBOOK FOR GiRLS

christian art kids

THE BiBLE STORYBOOK FOR girLS

Written by Phil Smouse
Illustrated by Amylee Weeks

The Bible Storybook for Girls
Copyright © 2015 by Christian Art Kids, an imprint of Christian Art Publishers,
PO Box 1599, Vereeniging, 1930, RSA

359 Longview Drive, Bloomingdale, IL 60108, USA

First edition 2015

Text copyright © 2015 by Phil A. Smouse. All rights reserved.
Art copyright © 2015 by Amylee Weeks. All rights reserved.

Scripture quotations are taken from the *Holy Bible*, New International Version® NIV®.
Copyright © 1973, 1978, 1984, 2011 by International Bible Society.
Used by permission of Biblica, Inc.® All rights reserved worldwide.

Scripture quotations are taken from the *New King James Version*.
Copyright © 1979, 1980, 1982 by Thomas Nelson, Inc.
Used by permission. All rights reserved.

Scripture quotations are taken from the *Holy Bible*, New Living Translation®.
Copyright © 1996, 2004, 2007, 2013 by Tyndale House Foundation.
Used by permission of Tyndale House Publishers, Inc., Carol Stream, Illinois 60188.
All rights reserved.

Printed in China

ISBN 978-1-4321-2051-1

15   16   17   18   19   20   21   22   23   24   –   10   9   8   7   6   5   4   3   2   1

dedications

For J.W., M.R., and our beautiful little Sophie . . .
Right from the beginning, God had a plan!
- Phil A. Smouse -

For Ryan, Morgan and Ashley . . .
So very grateful that God's plan for me
included each of you.
- Amylee Weeks -

❀contents❀

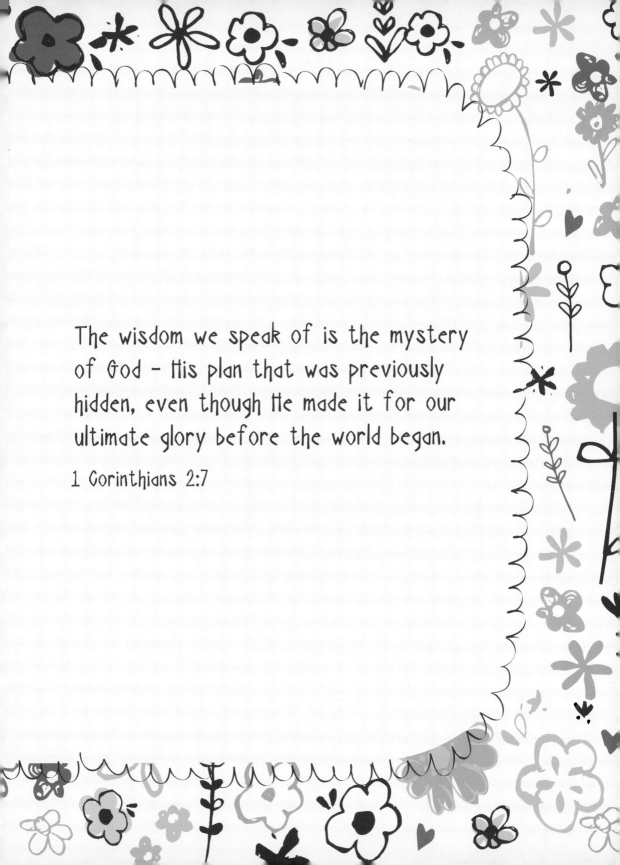

The wisdom we speak of is the mystery of God – His plan that was previously hidden, even though He made it for our ultimate glory before the world began.

1 Corinthians 2:7

Butterflies have a beautiful story to tell.

Their lives speak softly but powerfully of God's amazing love and the lengths He will go to take a small, often unattractive and seemingly worthless life, and unlock the incredible masterpiece heaven has hidden deep inside . . .

This story, the story of God's great love for us, is a story just like that.

Hidden among these pages are clues that reveal God's deep desire to unlock the heavenly masterpiece inside of all of us, and the incredible things God is willing to do to make sure that masterpiece will be revealed.

So let's start at the beginning . . .

13

CReATion

Genesis 1

Right from the beginning, God had a plan.

God made the world and everything in it.

God spoke and the sun, moon and stars came alive! The earth spun in sleepy blue circles of joy as He filled it with wonderful, beautiful things – floppy-eared bunnies, flowers and trees, and all of it filled with the heartbeat of heaven!

God made Adam and Eve.

18

adam and Eve

Genesis 1:24-27; 2:18-21

God looked at the world. He saw it was good. And so from the soft, swirling dust of the earth, as each snowflake and star gently sang out His praise, God whispered the names of His very first children, a man and a woman — Adam and Eve!

the garden of Eden

Genesis 2:8-17

20

God placed His children in a beautiful garden. He gave them every good thing their hearts desired.

And they were happy. "Everything I have is yours," God promised. "But you must not eat from the tree in the center of the garden."

So Adam and Eve did just as God said.

Adam and Eve loved God,
and God loved them.

They were free and alive
in the beautiful world God made . . .

Right from the beginning,
this was God's plan!

THE FORBIDDEN FRUIT

Genesis 3

But the devil hated Adam and Eve.
He hated God and the beautiful world
God made. So he became a serpent.
He tricked God's children!

"Did God really say you must not eat from the tree?" the serpent hissed. The serpent tricked Adam and Eve by tempting them to eat the fruit. He promised them it would make them happy.

So Adam and Eve bit into the fruit.

And suddenly there was a hole —
a missing piece — a piece they could
never put back again!

Did the fruit make them happy like
the serpent promised? No. It did
not! For now something was missing —
but not just in the fruit — there
was something missing in their hearts
as well.

And in that awful moment they knew — they would have to leave the garden and all the beautiful things God made — forever!

So the Lord placed an angel on the east side of Eden. A flaming sword blocked the road to the Tree of Life. The way back into God's beautiful garden seemed like it was closed for good.

cain and abel

Genesis 4:1-15

Many long, difficult years went by.
Adam worked and worked to find
the good things God gave them
so freely in the garden.

Adam's sons worked beside him.
Cain worked the ground. Abel looked
after the sheep.

Abel's heart was tender and kind.
He longed to know God. But Cain's
heart was as dark and hard and cold
 as the stony ground that they
fought to make their home.

Sin will drive your heart far away from God. You must learn to rule over it.

34

One day Abel went up to the fields with Cain. But Abel did not come home. Cain killed his brother!

"Where is Abel?" the Lord said to Cain.

"I don't know!" Cain replied angrily. "Am I my brother's keeper?"

Cain thought his clever words would outsmart God. But God saw the terrible thing Cain had done and banished him from his new home forever!

noah's ark

Genesis 6

The world became a terrible place!

God's heart was broken. Almost everyone was evil.

Noah was the only man left in all the world who still loved God with his whole heart.

So God told Noah to build an ark. He would send the animals two by two. For soon a flood would cover the earth and only Noah, his family and the animals on the ark would be saved!

God has a plan
to fix His broken world!

tHE flOOD

Genesis 7

It rained and rained for forty days and nights. The ark and everything in it was lifted high above the earth. Soon all the world – every rock, tree and mountain – was covered by the flood.

But the ark floated safely on the surface of the water.

tHe PROMISE

Genesis 8; 9:8–17

The flood washed away every living thing on the earth. But Noah and his family survived.

After many long, lonely months the ark came to rest on a mountain named Ararat.

One day Noah released a tiny white dove. She came back with an olive branch in her beak. Noah knew it would soon be dry enough to leave the ark.

Our mistakes cannot and will not take away God's love.

11

So the Lord swept a beautiful rainbow across the sky — a sparkling, heavenly masterpiece to remind them forever!

"This rainbow is My promise to you," God said to Noah, "That the waters will never cover the earth again."

So Noah, his family and all of the animals left the ark. They set off down the mountain and spread out over all the earth.

God filled the world with goodness and beauty once again. And all of God's creatures were filled with joy!

ABRAHAM — fRieNd of God

Genesis 15:1-6; 21:1-2

46

Hundreds of long, happy years went by.
One night, a man named Abraham looked
up into the beautiful starry sky.

God spoke and promised Abraham that
he would be the father of a great
nation.

"How can this be?" Abraham asked.
"I am an old man — almost one hundred
years old! My wife Sarah is almost
that old, too."

But in spite of all this, Abraham
believed God.

And when God saw his faith, His heart
leapt with joy.

Nothing is too difficult for God.

Soon, Abraham and Sarah did have a son!

Sarah laughed with delight as she held him in her arms.

They named their son "Isaac".

He grew strong and tall.

And their lives were filled with God's goodness and love.

Isaac

Genesis 22

Abraham loved God. He was God's friend. Sarah and Isaac loved Him, too. One day God decided to test Abraham.

"Abraham," God said, "Take your son, your only son, the son who you love, and offer him to Me as a sacrifice."

Abraham was confused. "I don't understand," he thought. "But God knows best."

So he and Isaac set out to do as God said.

"We have wood for the fire, but where is the sacrifice?" Isaac asked his father.

Abraham's eyes filled with tears.

"Abraham," God's angel whispered, "Don't be afraid. God sees that you are willing to give Him everything. Now He will give every good thing He has to you!"

Abraham dried his eyes and behold, there was a lamb for the sacrifice caught in a thicket.

Abraham and Isaac gave thanks to God with all of their hearts, then bowed down and worshipped Him there.

God will always keep His promises.

53

God hears our prayers.

Isaac and Rebekah

Genesis 25:19-26

Isaac grew into a man after God's heart. He married a beautiful girl named Rebekah. Abraham was proud of his son.

Isaac and Rebekah wanted to have a baby. They prayed and prayed.

♥ God heard their prayers. ♥

He gave them two sons – two twin sons! The babies danced inside of Rebekah's tummy.

"There are two mighty nations inside of you!" God said to her.

Esau was born first. He was covered with red hair. His twin brother, Jacob, was born second, holding onto Esau's heel.

JACOB AND ESAU

Genesis 25:27-34

Esau became a skillful hunter, a man of the fields. Jacob was happy to stay at home among the tents.

Once, when Jacob was cooking some stew, Esau came in from the open country.

"Let me have some of that red stew!" Esau said.

"Hurry up! I'm starving!"

Jacob knew that Esau was born first. He knew that Esau would get all of their family's land and animals when Isaac went to heaven.

But Jacob wanted those things for himself. So he decided to trick Esau!

"I see you are very hungry," Jacob said. "I will give you some stew. But first, give me your birthright!"

"I am about to die," Esau said angrily. "I don't care about that now. Just give me something to eat!"

But Jacob said, "No! Give me your birthright first!"

So Esau swore an oath, promising his birthright to Jacob. Then Jacob gave Esau some bread and red stew.

Esau ate and drank, and then got up and left.

Esau was very angry when he thought about what Jacob had done. But it was too late. Now Jacob would get everything!

God knows the secrets we try so hard to keep.

59

Jacob tricks Esau again

Genesis 27

One day, when Isaac was very old and his eyes began to grow dim, he called for his son Esau.

"I am an old man," Isaac said, "and I am about to die.

"Please, my son, go out to the open country and hunt some wild game. Make the delicious food I love and bring it to me.

"You are my firstborn son. I want to give you my blessing while I still can."

Jacob's mother, Rebekah, was listening as Isaac spoke to Esau. When Esau left for the open country, Rebekah said to Jacob, "I heard what your father said to Esau. Now listen carefully and do what I say. Make some delicious food for Isaac. Make it just the way he likes it. Then take it to him so he will give YOU his blessing before he dies!"

"Mother," Jacob said, "Esau is a hairy man. What if Father touches me? He'll know we are trying to trick him and take away Esau's blessing!"

But Jacob did just as his mother said . . . He gave Isaac the food. And Isaac gave Jacob the blessing!

63

Soon Esau came in from hunting. He made some delicious food and brought it to his father.

"Father, come! Sit up and eat!" Esau said happily, "so you may give me your blessing."

"Who are you?" Isaac asked warily.

"I am your firstborn son," Esau answered.

When Isaac heard this he began to tremble violently! "I ate just a few minutes ago! Who brought that food? I blessed someone else by mistake!"

Jacob's terrible trick filled Esau's heart with anger!

Rebekah heard what happened. She sent for Jacob and said, "Your brother, Esau, is planning to kill you. Listen carefully and do what I say. Flee at once! Go to my brother Laban. Stay there until Esau's fury subsides!"

So Jacob packed up and left that very night!

A dark, tangled heart creates a dark, tangled life.

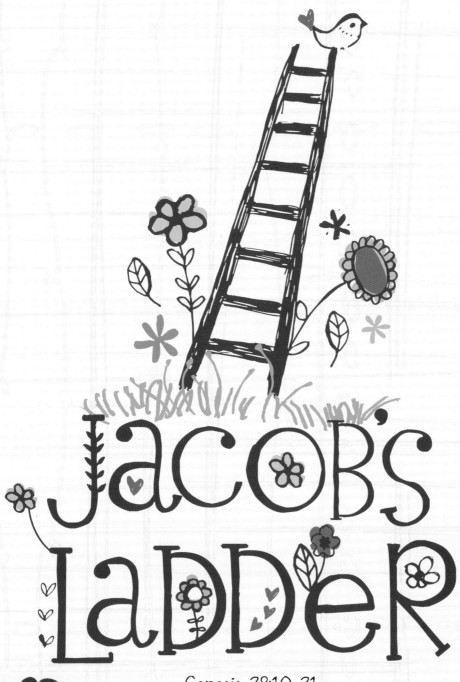

JACOB'S LADDER

Genesis 28:10–21

Yes, Jacob made many terrible mistakes. His choices hurt many people for a very long time.

But God loved Jacob. He loved him more than all of his mistakes.

Jacob left his home and his family and set out to find his Uncle Laban.

The journey was difficult and long. Jacob was exhausted. The sun was finally beginning to set. So Jacob found a stone and put it under his head for a pillow. Soon he was fast asleep.

That night Jacob had a dream. He saw a stairway resting on the earth. Its top reached into heaven. Angels danced up and down the stairway. And there at the very top, stood the Lord Himself!

"Jacob," the heavens thundered, "I am the God of Abraham and the God of your father, Isaac. I am with you. I will watch over you wherever you go. I will bring you back to your homeland. I will never leave you or take My love away. That is My promise."

Then Jacob arose from his sleep, and said, "Surely the Lord is in this place. He has been right here beside me all along and I did not even know it!"

God is with us whether we believe it or not.

69

People you love and trust will sometimes hurt you.

JACOB and RACHEL

Genesis 29:10–30

Jacob arrived at the home of his Uncle Laban. There he saw a well, and beside the well, three flocks of fuzzy white sheep sleeping happily.

Jacob rolled the stone away from the top of the well and began to water his uncle's thirsty sheep. Laban's daughter Rachel came and saw him there.

♥ It was love at first sight. ♥ Jacob kissed Rachel and began to weep for joy.

"Uncle Laban," Jacob said, "I will work for you for seven years if you let me marry Rachel."

So Jacob served Laban for seven long years. But they seemed like only a few days to him because he loved Rachel with all of his heart.

God will turn hurt into something good.

But when the time came for Jacob to marry Rachel, Laban decided to trick Jacob. He gave Jacob his daughter Leah instead!

"What have you done to me?" Jacob cried angrily. "I served you for seven years! Why did you deceive me?"

But Laban did not care. "The younger daughter does not get married before the older!" Laban laughed. "You may marry Rachel. But you must agree to work for me for another seven years!"

And because Jacob loved Rachel with all of his heart, he did exactly as Laban said. Jacob and Rachel were finally married. Soon their home was filled with a dozen happy children!

Jacob's New Name

Genesis 32–33

Jacob loved Esau. He wanted to be friends again. But he was afraid Esau would still be angry.

So Jacob prayed and prayed, then set out to find his brother.

The day was soon past — and the stars began to shine. The night was dark and and alive and beautiful!

But Jacob could not sleep. He thought he was alone . . . But NO! Someone was there in the darkness!

He fought and fought with a mysterious man, wrestling until the sun came up the next day!

The powerful stranger touched Jacob's hip. He wrenched it out of place! But Jacob fought on.

"Let Me go!" the stranger sang. "No!" Jacob replied. "I will not let You go unless You bless me!"

"What is your name?" the powerful stranger asked.

"My name is Jacob," he replied.

"Jacob?" the stranger cried in a voice that seemed to thunder from every star in the sky.

"Your name is no longer Jacob! Your new name is Israel, for you have struggled with God and with men and have overcome!"

The sun climbed higher into the sky. Jacob looked everywhere, but the stranger was gone.

Jacob's name was Israel — "God prevails"!

And because God prevails, Jacob and Esau did become friends again. Jacob's twelve sons grew and had families of their own. And those twelve sons and their families became the twelve tribes of Israel — God's chosen people — like the beautiful stars Abraham saw so many years ago!

God is not slow in keeping His promises!

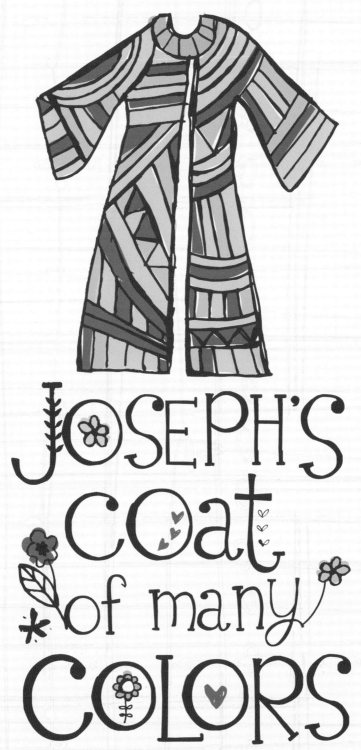

JOSEPH'S COAT of many COLORS

Genesis 37

Israel loved Joseph more than all of his other sons because Joseph was born when Israel was a very old man. So Israel made Joseph a beautiful coat of many colors.

When his brothers saw the coat, they became furious!

They were so jealous that they began to hate Joseph and would not speak a kind word to him.

One night Joseph had a dream.

"Brothers, listen!" Joseph said.
"Here is my dream! We were binding
sheaves of wheat out in the field
when suddenly my sheaf arose and
stood upright, while your sheaves
gathered around and bowed down
to it."

When his brothers heard this, they
hated him even more! "Do you really
think you will be our king?" they
roared.

At first, even Israel was angry and
surprised. But deep in his heart, he
wondered if it might be true.

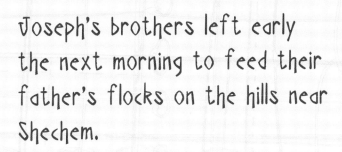

Joseph's brothers left early
the next morning to feed their
father's flocks on the hills near
Shechem.

"Here comes that dreamer!"
they said to each other when
they saw Joseph coming near.

"Let's kill him and throw him
into one of these wells. We'll
tell Israel that a ferocious
animal devoured him. Then we'll
see what comes of his dreams!"

"No!" shouted Joseph's brother
Reuben. "We must not take his
life. Throw him into this well,
but don't lay a hand on him."

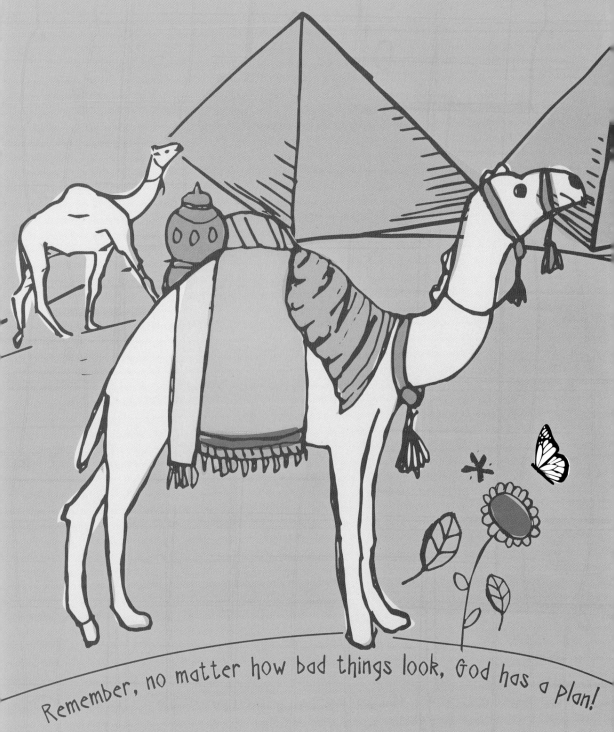

Remember, no matter how bad things look, God has a plan!

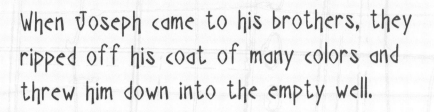

When Joseph came to his brothers, they ripped off his coat of many colors and threw him down into the empty well.

As Joseph's brothers sat down to eat their meal, they looked up and saw a caravan of merchants.

Their camels were loaded down with spices, for they were on their way to Egypt.

"Let's sell him to these men!" they said to one another. "After all, he is our brother!" So his brothers all agreed, and when the merchants came by, they pulled Joseph up out of the well and sold him for twenty pieces of silver.

Then the merchants took Joseph and set off for Egypt.

JOSEPH in Egypt

Genesis 39:1-4, 7-27

Pharaoh was the king of Egypt. His servant Potiphar was in charge of all the king's men.

Potiphar bought Joseph from the slave traders, and put Joseph to work in his house.

But the Lord was with Joseph. He lived in the house of his Egyptian master. Everything he did prospered.

When Potiphar saw that the Lord was with him, and that God gave Joseph success in everything he did, he put Joseph in charge of everything he owned!

God's way is always the right way, even when things go wrong.

Now, Joseph was strong and very handsome.

Potiphar's wife began to fall in love with him. But Joseph would not fall in love with the wife of another man. So Potiphar's wife became very angry.

"Help!" she cried out, "this man tried to hurt me!"

But Joseph did not try to hurt her. Potiphar's wife lied, and the king's guards believed her!

They came and carried Joseph away and threw him into prison.

God knows what we do not know.

JOSEPH in PRISON

Genesis 40

Joseph was in prison for a very long time. But God was with him, even there.

When the chief jailer saw how God took care of Joseph, he put him in charge of the entire prison.

And God gave him success in everything he did.

One day, one of the prisoners had a terrible dream. He wondered what it could mean.

So he came to Joseph and asked him.

"I cannot tell you," Joseph replied, "but God can. Now come and tell me your dream."

God sees what we cannot see.

91

"In my dream I saw a vine," the man said.

"The vine had three branches. Its branches blossomed, and ripened into grapes. Pharaoh's cup was in my hand. I took the grapes, squeezed them into Pharaoh's cup, and put the cup in his hand."

"The three branches are three days," Joseph said.

"In three days you will be set free from this prison. You will give the king his cup, just as you did before."

"Thank you!" the man replied. "How can I ever repay you?"

"Please remember me when you are free," Joseph said kindly. "Perhaps Pharaoh will let me out of this prison."

Three days later, on Pharaoh's birthday, there was a huge party. The cupbearer was set free, just as Joseph said.

But he did not remember Joseph. He forgot about him! And Joseph stayed there in prison for another two long years!

PHARAOH'S DREAM

Genesis 41:1-49

Then, after two long, lonely years, Pharaoh had a dream!

He dreamed that he was standing by the Nile River. Seven healthy, fat cows came up and grazed among the reeds. Then seven thin, hungry cows came and stood beside them.

Pharaoh's mind was troubled. He wondered what it could mean. He sent for his magicians, but they could not help him.

The next morning, the king's cup-bearer remembered Joseph.

So Pharaoh sent for Joseph. He was set free from prison and brought before the king.

Pharaoh told Joseph his terrible dream.

"Tell me, Joseph, what does it mean?" the king asked.

"I cannot tell you," Joseph replied, "but God can."

"The seven fat cows are seven good years. The seven thin cows are seven years of terrible hunger!"

Then Pharaoh said to Joseph, "Since God made all this known to you, you shall be in charge of my palace, and all of my people are to do as you say."

So the king put Joseph in charge of all the land. For seven long years, Joseph worked hard to store away food for the years of terrible hunger that were coming.

And God gave Joseph success in everything he did.

God can do what we cannot do!

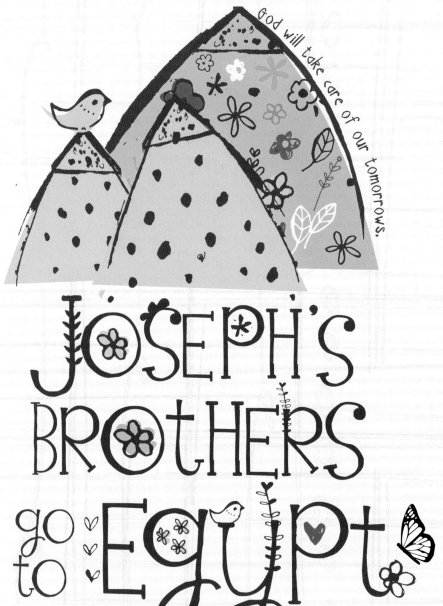

God will take care of our tomorrows.

JOSEPH'S BROTHERS go to EGYPT

Genesis 42–44

Soon the seven years of terrible hunger were upon the land. The only food anywhere was the food Joseph had stored in Egypt!

When Israel learned that there was food in Egypt, he said, "My sons, go down to Egypt. Buy us some grain that we may live and not die!"

So ten of Joseph's brothers went down to Egypt. But Israel would not send Benjamin, Joseph's youngest brother, because he was afraid something might happen to Benjamin on the journey.

Joseph's brothers arrived and bowed down before him. Joseph recognized his brothers, but they did not recognize him!

So Joseph pretended to be a stranger. He spoke angrily to them. "Where did you come from?" he asked.

"From the land of Canaan," they replied, "to buy food."

"You are spies!" Joseph said.

"No!" his brothers insisted.

"No!" Joseph replied. "You are spies. And you will never go back home unless your youngest brother comes here!

"Now go! Send one brother to get him. Until then, the rest of you will be kept in prison."

"Surely we are being punished because of what we did to Joseph!" they said to one another. So Simeon went home to Israel.

After many days he returned with Benjamin and they stood before Joseph again.

"How is your father?" Joseph asked.

"Our father is alive and well," they replied.

"Is this your youngest brother?" Joseph asked.

"Yes," they replied.

But when Joseph saw Benjamin, his heart was filled with emotion. He left his brothers and wept because of all that had happened.

"Fill the men's sacks with as much food as they can carry," Joseph said to his servent.

"Put each brother's money into the top of each sack. Then put my own silver cup into Benjamin's sack, along with the money for his grain."

And he did as Joseph said.

A human heart is a fragile thing.

107

When morning came, Joseph sent his brothers on their way. After a short time, he sent his servant out after them.

"Why have you stolen from my master?" Joseph's servant asked. Then he tore open their sacks and they saw the bags of coins and the silver cup in Benjamin's sack. "We didn't do it!" they cried. "Yes, you did! And now you will ALL be slaves of my master!" Joseph's servant thundered.

But when Joseph saw them, he said, "No! Only the man who had my silver cup will become my slave. The rest of you, go back to your father in peace."

"No!" they all cried. "Please, no! That would break our father's heart!"

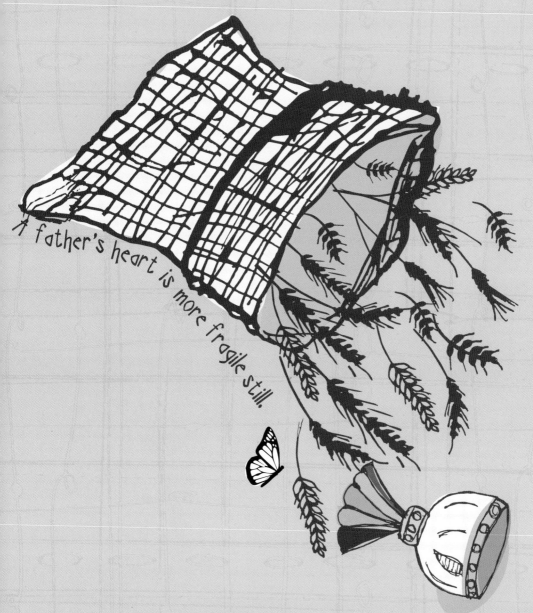

A father's heart is more fragile still.

When we love God, all things work together for our good.

JOSEPH'S BROTHERS BOW DOWN

Genesis 45

Joseph's brothers were terrified.

"Come, gather around," he said to them. "I am your brother Joseph, the one you sold into slavery. Do not be afraid. God sent me ahead of you! For two years there has been terrible hunger in the land. And for the next five years there will be hunger still.

Don't you see . . . God sent me here to save your lives — to save OUR lives — and that's exactly what He has done!"

"Now go! Hurry back to our father and say to him, 'This is what your son Joseph says: God has made me master of all Egypt. Come now. Do not delay. You shall live in the land of Egypt and be near me — you, your children and grandchildren, your flocks and herds, and all you have. And I will provide for you there!'"

A godless heart is filled with anger and fear.

GOD'S CHILDREN BECOME SLAVES

Exodus 1:8–14

Many years went by. For a time, God's children lived happily in Egypt – until a new king came to power – a king who did not care about Joseph or God's people.

"The Israelites have become far too powerful," the king said roughly. "We must do something to stop them before they rise up against us and try to leave the country."

So the new king put slave masters over God's children. They were forced to work night and day in the burning desert to build great cities of brick and stone for Pharaoh.

God can mend the trouble an angry heart brings.

THE BIRTH of moses

Exodus 1:22–2:10

Pharaoh hated God's children. He ordered his servants to kill every baby boy born to God's people!

One day, a beautiful young woman named Jochebed gave birth to a son. She hid him for three months.

When she could hide him no longer, she made a little basket and coated it with tar.

She placed her baby in the basket and hid it among the reeds along the bank of the Nile. Her daughter stood at a distance to see what would happen to her baby brother!

Pharaoh's daughter went down to the Nile. She saw the basket among the reeds.

When she opened the basket, she saw the baby. He was crying! Her heart was broken. She knew why the baby was there.

"Shall I go and get one of the Hebrew women to take care of the baby?" a tiny voice said from somewhere among the reeds. "Yes, go," Pharaoh's daughter answered.

So the girl, who was hiding, went and got the baby's mother! When the child grew older, his mother took him to Pharaoh's daughter and he became her son.

So she named him Moses, saying, "I drew him out of the water."

God sees every good thing we do. He sees every bad thing, too.

moses in EGYPT

118

Exodus 2:11-24

Many years later, after Moses had grown up, he went out to where God's children lived.

He watched as they slaved to build Pharaoh's city. Moses saw an Egyptian beating a Hebrew. His heart burned with anger! He looked this way and that.

And when he saw that no one was watching, he killed the Egyptian and hid him in the sand!

When Pharaoh heard of this, he tried to kill Moses.

But Moses fled from Pharaoh and went to live in Midian.

God will find a way to fix the bad things.

Moses was happy in Midian and decided to stay. He married a beautiful woman named Zipporah.

Soon they had a strong son. Moses named him Gershom, which means, "I am a stranger in a strange land."

Many long years went by. The king of Egypt died. God's children cried out day and night to be delivered from their terrible life of slavery.

God heard their cries. He remembered the promise He made to Abraham and decided to send someone to save them.

tHE BuRNing BuSH

Exodus 3

One day, as Moses was tending his father-in-law's sheep, an angel of the Lord appeared to him in flames of fire from within a burning bush.

"This is a very strange sight!" Moses thought.

"The bush is on fire, but it does not burn up!"

So he came closer to take a look.

God is holy.

"Moses! Moses!" God called from within the burning bush.

"Here I am," Moses replied.

"Do not come any closer," God said. "Take off your shoes, for the place where you are standing is holy ground.

"I am the God of your father, the God of Abraham, the God of Isaac and the God of Jacob."

When Moses heard this, he hid his face. He was afraid to look at God!

God longs to save His children!

"I have seen the misery of My people in Egypt," the Lord said to Moses. "I have heard them crying out for help. Their terrible suffering is breaking My heart.

"So I have come to rescue them from the Egyptians. I will bring them up out of that land into a good land – a land that flows with milk and honey.

"So go. I am sending YOU to Pharaoh to bring My people, the Israelites, out of Egypt."

Pride always goes before a fall.

Let my people go

Exodus 5:1–8

So Moses and his brother Aaron went to Pharaoh and said, "This is what the Lord, the God of Israel, says:

'Let My people go, so that they may worship Me in the wilderness!'"

"Who is the Lord," Pharaoh said, "that I should obey Him? I do not know the Lord and I will not let Israel go."

So Pharaoh ordered the slave drivers and overseers to take away the straw God's children needed to make bricks!

"Let them go and gather their own straw!" Pharaoh roared, "but see that they make the same number of bricks as before!"

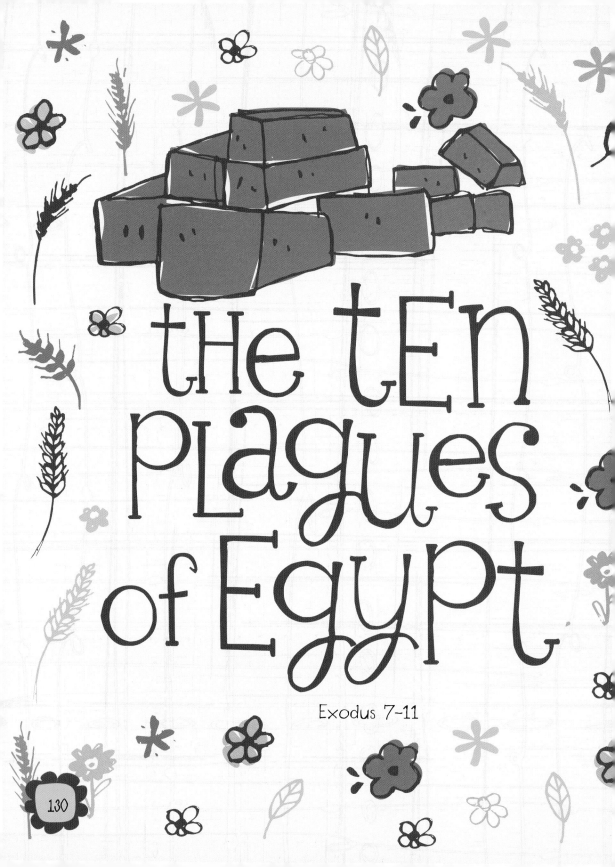

tHE tEN plaguES of Egypt

Exodus 7–11

So God's children made bricks without straw!

But God hardened Pharaoh's heart. He would not let them go.

"Pharaoh will not listen to you," the Lord said to Moses.

"And now, because he will not, My wonders will be seen in Egypt!"

So the Lord sent ten terrible plagues on the land!

The Plague of Blood

The Plague of Frogs

The Plague of Gnats

The Plague of Flies

The Plague on Livestock

The Plague of Boils

The Plague of Hail

The Plague of Locusts

The Plague of Darkness

God's name is the name above every name in heaven and on earth.

Then the Lord said to Moses, "I will bring one more plague on Pharaoh and his people. After that, he will let you go."

So Moses stood before Pharaoh and said, "This is what the Lord says: 'At about midnight, I will go throughout Egypt. Every firstborn son in the land will die, including the son of Pharaoh!

'But among My children, not one person will be harmed. Not even a dog will bark. Then you will know that the Lord takes care of those who love Him!'"

Our God is an awesome God.

THE PASSOVER

Exodus 12:1–30

So the Lord told Moses to tell all of God's children that on the tenth day of that month each man was to take a lamb for his family, one for each household.

Then they were to take some of the blood and put it on the sides and tops of the doorframes of their houses.

"On the night I pass through Egypt," God told them, "I will strike down the firstborn of Egypt – both man and animals, for I am the Lord. The blood will be a sign for you! When I see the blood, I will pass over you. No harm will come to you when I strike Egypt."

And that is exactly what God did.

tHE eXOdUS

Exodus 12:31–51; 13

During the night, Pharaoh called for Moses and said, "Go! Leave my people! Take your flocks and herds.

"Worship the Lord as you have asked. Hurry!

"Leave quickly before everyone in Egypt is no more!"

139

So God's children left Egypt.

By day the Lord went ahead of them in a pillar of clouds.

By night He moved in a pillar of fire to give them light!

The pillars of clouds and fire never left their place in front of God's people. God led them safely out of Egypt.

THE RED SEA

Exodus 14:5-31

When Pharaoh heard that God's people had fled, his heart was hardened once again. "What have we done?" he thundered. So he had his chariot made ready and set out with his army to destroy God's children once and for all.

The Israelites marched out of Egypt with great joy.

But Pharaoh's army – his horses and chariots, his horsemen and troops – overtook them as they camped by the Red Sea!

"Do not be afraid!" Moses shouted. "Stand firm and you will see God deliver us today! The Lord will fight for us! All we need to do is be still and know that He is God!"

Then Moses stretched out his hand over the sea. All that night the Lord drove the sea back with a strong east wind.

The waters divided and God's people went through the sea on dry ground, with a wall of water on their right and a wall of water on their left!

God's creation obeys when it hears His voice!

But still the Egyptians chased after them! All of Pharaoh's horses, chariots and horsemen followed God's people into the sea.

So the Lord looked down from inside the pillar of fire and filled the hearts of the Egyptians with terror and fear!

He jammed the wheels of their chariots so they could not move.

"Let's get away from here!" they shrieked. "The Lord Himself is fighting against us!"

147

Then the Lord said to Moses, "Stretch out your hand over the sea.

"Let the waters flow back over the Egyptians and their army."

So Moses stretched out his hand over the sea, and the water swept away Pharaoh and his army. Not one of them survived!

When the Israelites saw the mighty hand of the Lord, they put their trust in God and in Moses his servant.

Those who love God will see His power with their very own eyes.

149

If we are listening, God will always tell us exactly what to do.

tHE tEN commanDmENts

Exodus 19-20

On the first day of the third month after God's children left Egypt, they came to the desert of Sinai and camped there in front of God's mountain.

The mountain was covered with smoke.

The Lord descended on it in fire!

The sound of a mighty trumpet grew louder and louder as the mountain began to shake!

Then the Lord called Moses up to the top of the mountain and there God spoke these words . . .

"I am the Lord your God, who brought you out of Egypt.

"You shall have no other god but Me.

"You shall not make for yourself an idol in the shape of anything in heaven or earth. You shall not bow down to worship them.

152

"You shall not misuse the name of the Lord your God.

"Remember the Sabbath day by keeping it holy.

"Honor your father and your mother, so you may live long in the land that I am giving you.

"You shall not murder.

"You shall not fall in love with anyone other than your own husband or wife.

"You shall not steal.

"You shall not lie.

"You shall not long to have your neighbor's house, your neighbor's wife, or anything that belongs to him."

153

So God's people did exactly as He said . . . for a little while.

As the years went by, God's beautiful garden became a distant memory. It seemed so long ago that most people weren't even sure it really happened.

They knew God's commandments.

They knew they were supposed to keep them.

But life went on as it always had.

Some days it feels like God's love is nowhere to be found.

RutH

Ruth 1:1–21

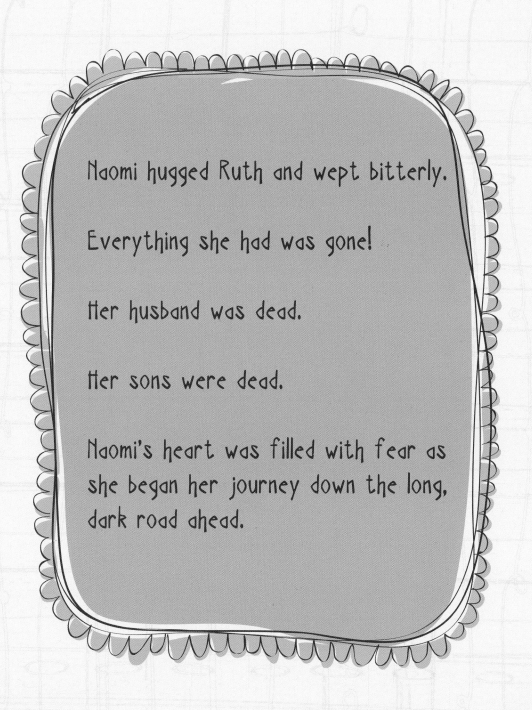

Naomi hugged Ruth and wept bitterly.

Everything she had was gone!

Her husband was dead.

Her sons were dead.

Naomi's heart was filled with fear as she began her journey down the long, dark road ahead.

"Ruth," Naomi cried. "You must go home. I love you. But I am an old woman. Without our husbands we will die here too."

"No!" Ruth wept. "I cannot leave you. I will go where you go. I will stay where you stay. Your God will be my God. He will find a way to turn our darkness into songs of joy."

Bethlehem – Home at Last

Ruth 1:2-4:16

Ruth and Naomi climbed down
from their little donkey.
Naomi's friends ran to greet
them — a welcome blessing for
two broken hearts longing for
home.

"Let me go into the fields,"
Ruth begged.

"I'll gather the grain the
farmers leave behind."

But oh, when she did . . .

161

"Who is that girl?" the farm owner asked.
"What is she doing on my land? Bring her
here!"

Naomi could not believe her ears. Boaz, the
farm owner, was a member of her family!
He became Ruth's husband and took care of
Ruth and Naomi for the rest of their lives.

But even in our most difficult times, God is working for our good.

163

David and goliath

1 Samuel 17:1-54

The army of God was frozen with fear.

Goliath, one of the enemy, was over nine feet tall. His weapons of war were even bigger than that.

"Come out and fight!" the giant roared.

But nobody moved – until little David appeared.

166

Was David afraid? No! Goliath was big.

But God was bigger.

"Come and get it!" Goliath laughed as he moved in for the kill. But it was too late. Out came David's sling; in went the stone.

Bop!

Goliath crashed to the ground before he even knew what hit him!

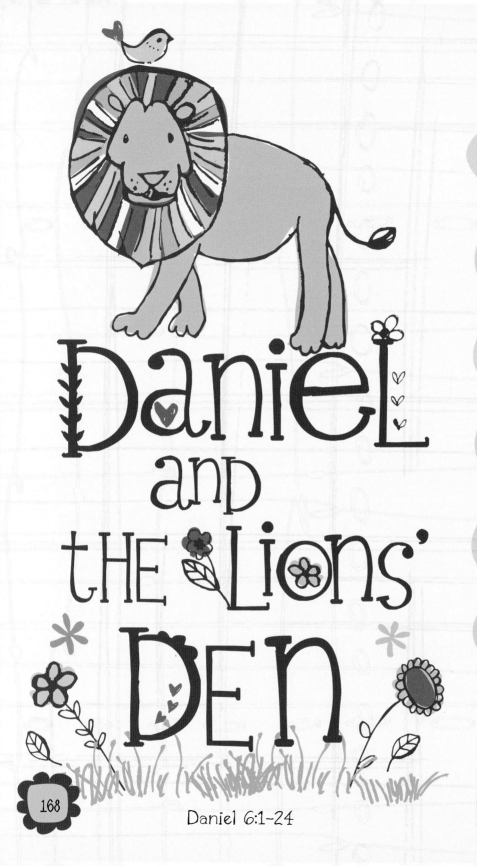

Daniel and the Lions' Den

Daniel 6:1-24

Daniel loved God. He worked hard. He always did the right thing.

All the king's men hated him for it. So they set a trap. They tricked the king! He signed their new law – if you pray to God, you will be thrown into a den of hungry lions!

The very next day, Daniel was caught. The king was furious. He ran to the den!

"Daniel, are you all right?" he cried.

"Yes!" Daniel replied. "I'm praying with the lions. It's time for their breakfast."

So the king pulled Daniel out — and threw the men who tricked him into the den!

JonaH

Jonah 1–3

The word of the Lord came to Jonah.

"Go to the great city of Nineveh. Tell the people about My amazing love."

But Jonah did not go. He ran the other way!

Then he hid in the bottom of a boat and fell fast asleep.

A terrible storm arose.

The tiny ship was tossed! "It's all my fault," Jonah cried.

"Throw me out. The storm will stop!"

So over he went — into the ocean — where he was swallowed by a big fish!

"O Lord, forgive me," Jonah prayed as the fish spat him out.

And the people of Nineveh heard about the amazing love of God.

a Distant memory

Hundreds of years went by.

Once again, God's beautiful garden became nothing but a distant memory.

It seemed so long ago that most people weren't even sure it really happened.

Deep in their hearts they longed to get back to that beautiful place.

But no one seemed to know the way.

Until one day, when . . .

unto us a CHILD is BORN

Isaiah 9:6-7

The people who walked in
darkness have seen a great
light!

For unto us a Child is born.
Unto us a Son is given. And
the government will be upon
His shoulders.

His name will be called
Wonderful, Counselor, Mighty
God, Everlasting Father,
Prince of Peace.

Of the increase of His
kingdom and His peace, there
will be no end!

Unto us a Child is born!

THE bIRTH of JESUS

Luke 2:1-7; Matthew 1:18-25

The birth of Jesus happened like this:

In those days Caesar Augustus issued a decree that every person in the entire Roman world must return to their own town to be counted.

So Joseph went up from the town of Nazareth in Galilee to Bethlehem, the town of David. He went there to be counted with Mary. They would soon be married and were expecting a Child.

While they were there, the time came for the Baby to be born.

So Mary gave birth to a Son. She wrapped the Baby in cloth and placed Him in a manger, because there was no room for them in the inn.

Right from the beginning, God had a plan!

181

Yes, before they were married, Joseph knew that Mary was going to have a baby!

Joseph loved Mary. He did not want people to hate her for this. So he decided to leave her quietly, so no one would find out.

But an angel of the Lord appeared to him in a dream and said, "Do not be afraid to take Mary as your wife. The Baby inside her was put there by God Himself."

"Mary will give birth to a Son. You are to give Him the name Jesus, because He will save His people from their sins."

All this took place to fulfill what the Lord said many years ago: "The virgin will conceive and give birth to a Son, and they will call Him Immanuel which means God with us."

THE SHEPHERDS VISIT JESUS

Luke 2:8-20

There were shepherds living out in the fields nearby, keeping watch over their flocks.

An angel of the Lord appeared to them. The glory of the Lord shone all around them and they were very afraid!

But the angel said to them, "Fear not! I bring you good news!

"Yes, great joy for all the people. Today in the city of David a Savior has been born to you; He is Christ, the Lord!

"And this will be a sign to you: You will find a Baby wrapped in cloth and lying in a manger."

Suddenly a great company of the heavenly host appeared with the angel, praising God and saying, "Glory to God in the highest and on earth peace to those on whom His favor rests."

So the shepherds hurried off and found Mary, Joseph and the Baby, who was lying in the manger.

They told everyone everywhere what they had seen. All who heard it were amazed at what the shepherds said.

Mary treasured up all these things and pondered them in her heart.

And the shepherds returned home, praising God for all the things they had heard and seen, which happened just as they had been told it would so very long ago!

SiMEON

Luke 2:1-35, 39-40

Eight days later, Joseph and Mary named their Baby Jesus — the name He was given by the angel before Mary even knew that He would be born!

They brought Him to the temple in Jerusalem to thank God and present Him to the Lord.

Now there was a man in Jerusalem whose name was Simeon. Simeon was a good man who loved God.

God's Holy Spirit was upon him.

He came into the temple, and when Joseph and Mary brought in the Child, Simeon took Him up in his arms, thanked God and said, "Lord, now I can depart in peace, for my eyes have seen Your salvation — the One You have sent to save Your people from their sins!"

So Joseph, Mary and Jesus went back to Galilee, to their own town of Nazareth.

And the Child grew and became strong. He was filled with wisdom, and the favor of God was upon Him.

THE WiSE MEN ViSiT JESUS

Matthew 2:1-12

191

In the days of King Herod, after Jesus was born, wise men from the east came looking for a king!

"Where is the One they call King of the Jews?" the wise men asked. "We saw His star and have come to worship Him."

When King Herod heard this, his heart was filled with fear! "Where is this Savior to be born?" the king asked his priests. "In Bethlehem," they replied, "Just as the prophets said long, long ago."

So King Herod decided to meet the wise men secretly to find out when the star had appeared, and to learn what the wise men knew about the Child.

King Herod sent the wise men to Bethlehem and said, "Go and search for the Child. When you find Him, tell me where He is, so that I may go and worship Him, too."

But Herod did not want to worship Jesus. Herod wanted to kill Him!

So the wise men went on their way.

The star they saw in the east went ahead of them and stopped over the place where the Child lived!

When they finally came to the house, their hearts were filled with joy! They saw Jesus with His mother, Mary.

The wise men bowed down and worshipped Him and gave Him gifts of gold, frankincense and myrrh.

Then, having been warned in a dream not to go back to Herod, they returned to their country by another way!

Escape to Egypt

Matthew 2:13-20

After the wise men had gone home, an angel appeared to Joseph in a dream.

"Get up!" the angel said, "take the Child and His mother and flee to Egypt. Stay there until I tell you to come home, for King Herod is going to try to find your Child and kill Him!"

So Joseph got up. He took Mary and the Baby during the night and left for Egypt.

When Herod found out that he had been tricked by the wise men, he became very angry.

He ordered his men to kill every boy in Bethlehem who was two years old or younger.

But Joseph and his family lived safely in Egypt until Herod died, and then they returned home.

So the words that the prophet spoke long ago came to pass once again: "Out of Egypt I have called My Son."

Jesus in the temple

Luke 2:41-52

When Jesus was twelve years old, He and His family went up to Jerusalem for the Festival of the Passover, just like they did every year since they returned home.

After the festival was over, Mary and Joseph began the long journey home. But Jesus stayed behind in Jerusalem.

Thinking Jesus was with them, Mary and Joseph traveled on for an entire day before they realized He was missing!

They began looking for Him among their relatives and friends. But they could not find Him!

So they hurried back to Jerusalem to look for Jesus there.

After three days they found Jesus in the temple, sitting among the teachers, listening to them and asking them questions. Everyone who heard Jesus was amazed at His wisdom.

But when His parents found Him, they were upset and surprised. "Son, why have You treated us like this?"

His mother said, "Your father and I have been searching for You everywhere!"

"Why were you searching for Me?" Jesus asked. "Didn't you know I would be in My Father's house, about My Father's business?"

JESUS is tESTED in tHE wilDERNESS

Matthew 4:1–11

Many years later, when Jesus had grown up and become a man, He was led by God's Spirit into the wilderness to be tested by the devil.

After fasting for forty days and forty nights, Jesus became very hungry. So the devil came to Him and said, "If You are the Son of God, tell these stones to become bread!"

Jesus answered, "It is written: 'Man cannot live on bread alone. He must learn to live on every word that comes from the mouth of God.'"

Satan tempted Jesus just like he tempted Adam, Eve and everyone else. But Jesus did not sin.

So the devil took Jesus to the top of a very high mountain. He showed Jesus the wealth and power of all the kingdoms of the world. "I will give this all to You," the devil said, "if You will bow down and worship me!"

"Get away from Me, Satan!" Jesus said. "For it is written: 'Worship the Lord your God, and serve Him only.'"

So the devil left Him, and angels came and cared for Him there.

Water into wine

John 2:1–11

One day a wedding took place at Cana in Galilee. Jesus' mother was there. Jesus and His disciples had been invited as well. When the wine was finished, Jesus' mother said to Him, "They have no more wine."

"Mother, why are you asking Me to do this?" Jesus replied.

But His mother said to the servants, "Do whatever Jesus tells you."

Six stone water jars stood nearby.

"Fill the jars with water," Jesus said to the servants. So they filled them all the way to the top. "Now pour some out and take it to the master of the banquet."

The master of the banquet tasted the water. He did not know that Jesus had turned it into wine!

Then he called for the bridegroom and said, "Most people bring out the best wine first, but you have saved the very best until now!"

This was the first miracle that Jesus did to reveal His glory, and His disciples believed in Him.

niCoDEMUS

John 3:1-17

You must be born again!

There once was a man named Nicodemus.

He was very religious. But his heart held a question that no one could answer — until he met Jesus.

"Master," Nicodemus whispered softly, "What must I do to get into heaven?"

"Nicodemus," Jesus replied, "unless you are born again, you cannot see the kingdom of God.

"Why are you so surprised? God loved the world so much He gave His only Son so that everyone who believes in Him will never die, but will live with God in heaven forever."

THE WOMAN at THE WELL

216

John 4:1-25

Jesus came to a town in Samaria near the place Jacob had given to his son Joseph so very long ago.

It was about noon and Jesus was tired from the long, hot journey. So He sat down next to Jacob's well to rest.

When a Samaritan woman came to draw water, Jesus said to her, "Will you please give Me a drink?"

"But you are a Jew and I am a Samaritan!" the woman said to Jesus. She was very surprised. "People like You do not waste their time with people like me."

Jesus came to save us from our sins.

"If you knew the gift God gave you, and who it is that asks you for a drink," Jesus replied, "you would have asked Me, and I would have given you living water!"

"I don't understand," the woman replied. "Everyone who drinks from this well will be thirsty again."

Jesus said softly, "But everyone who drinks the water I give will never be thirsty. For the water I give will flow through you like a river, giving you eternal life."

"Sir, give me this water!" The woman said to Jesus, "for I know that the Messiah is coming to save us from our sins."

Then Jesus looked at her with tenderness and great joy and said, "I AM the Messiah!"

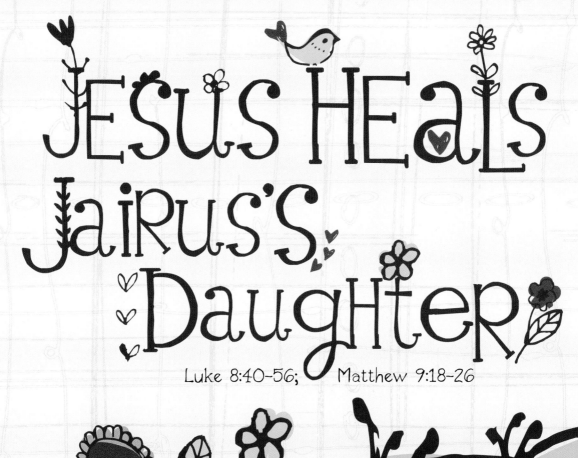

JESUS HEALS JAIRUS'S DAUGHTER

Luke 8:40-56; Matthew 9:18-26

Jesus crossed over to the other side of a lake. A large crowd gathered around Him there.

One of the religious leaders, a man named Jairus, was in the crowd. When Jairus saw Jesus, he fell at His feet and said, "Please help me! My little daughter is dying. Come and put Your hands on her so that she will be healed and live again."

So Jesus followed Jairus back to his house.

A large crowd followed them and pressed in all around.

There was a woman in the crowd who had been bleeding for twelve years. She suffered a great deal and spent all she had on many doctors.

But instead of getting better, she grew worse and worse.

When she saw Jesus, she came up behind Him and touched His cloak. "If I could just touch His clothes, I will be healed." she thought.

So that is what she did!

And the minute she touched Him, her bleeding stopped. She was free from her suffering!

At once Jesus realized that power had gone out from Him. "Who touched Me?" Jesus asked the people around Him.

Then the woman came and fell at Jesus' feet. Trembling with fear, she told Him the whole truth.

"Daughter," Jesus said gently, "go in peace. Your faith has healed you."

Jesus has the power over death and life.

While Jesus was still speaking, some people came from Jairus's house. "Jairus, your daughter is dead!" they said. But Jesus heard them and said, "Don't be afraid, Jairus; just believe."

When they came to Jairus's home, Jesus saw the people crying and wailing loudly. "Why are you all crying?" He asked. "The child is not dead. She is only sleeping."

When the people heard this they laughed at Jesus!

So He went into her room, took her by the hand and said, "Little girl, get up." And that is exactly what she did.

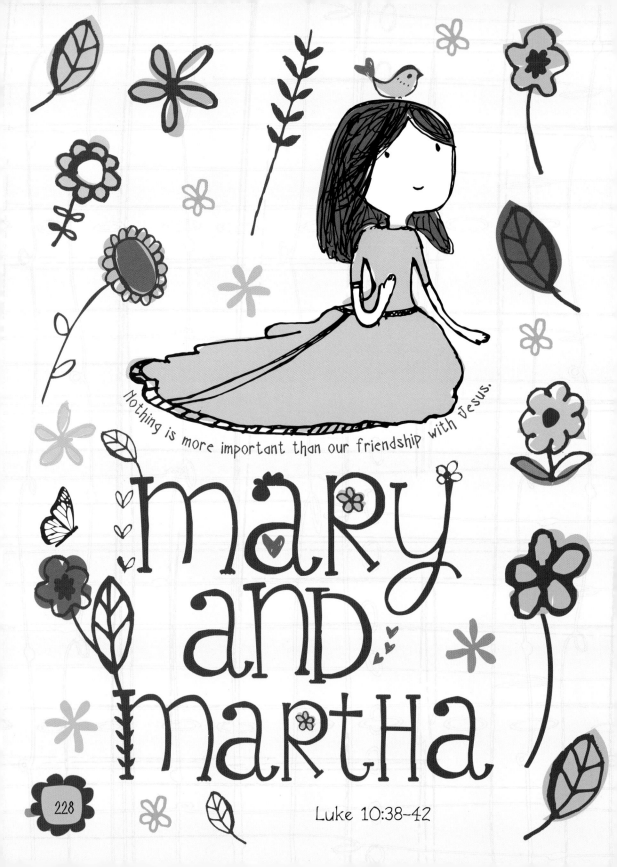

Nothing is more important than our friendship with Jesus.

MARY AND MARTHA

Luke 10:38-42

228

Jesus and His disciples went on their way. Soon they came to a village where a woman named Martha lived. She opened her home and welcomed them in. Martha had a sister named Mary.

Mary sat at Jesus' feet, listening to every word He said. But Martha was distracted by all the work she needed to do.

"Lord, don't You care that my sister has left me to do all the work by myself?" Martha asked. "Tell her to get up and help me!"

"Martha, Martha," Jesus answered, "you are worried and upset about many things. Mary has chosen what is better, and it will not be taken away from her."

Jesus came to seek and save the lost.

THE LOST SHEEP

Luke 15:4-7

230

Jesus said, "If a man has a hundred sheep and one of them wanders off, what will he do?

"Will he leave the others to look for the one who is lost?

"Of course! But when he finds her, will he be angry?

"No! He will carry her home with a thankful heart.

"Why? Because there is more joy in heaven over one lost sheep who finds her way home than for all of the others who never wandered away!"

THE PRODIGAL SON

Luke 15:11-24

Jesus will forgive all of our sins.

A certain man had two sons.

One day the younger son packed his bags and set out for a far country. There he spent everything he had on wild living.

The son began to starve! But no one would give him anything. So he gathered up his things and began the long journey home.

While he was still a long way off, the father saw him coming. The father's heart was filled with joy. He ran to meet his son.

"Bring my finest robe — a ring and sandals, too! My son was lost, but now he is found!"

Jesus is always right on time.

Lazarus, come forth!

John 11:1-44

"Lord, come quickly," the letter read. "Your friend Lazarus is very sick." But it was too late. Lazarus had already been dead for four long days!

"Roll away the gravestone," Jesus told the people.

"But, Lord," Lazarus's sister wept, "the smell will be terrible!"

"Martha," Jesus whispered. "Your brother will rise again."

Then He looked up to heaven, spread out His arms and cried, "Father, thank You for hearing Me. I know You always hear Me. Now, so everyone else will hear You and know You are God . . .

"Lazarus, come forth!"

And Lazarus did!

The religious man could only see the mistakes of others.

THE alaBasteR BOX

Matthew 26:6-13; Luke 7:44-50

One evening a very religious man invited Jesus to dinner. So Jesus went to his house and sat down at the table. A woman who lived nearby learned that Jesus had come.

She brought a beautiful alabaster box filled with perfume and knelt at Jesus' feet and wept, for she was a sinner. Her tears fell on His feet.

So she dried them with her hair.

Then she kissed His feet and poured the perfume on them.

The religious man saw this and mumbled, "If Jesus was really God, He would know what kind of sinful woman she is."

"I came to your house and you did
not give Me water to wash My feet,"
Jesus said to the religious man. "But
this woman washed My feet with her
tears and dried them with her hair!

"You did nothing to welcome Me. But
she has poured out every drop of
her finest perfume, for she loves
Me very much.

"Therefore I tell you, her many sins
have been forgiven!"

the sinful woman LOVED Jesus with all her heart

239

tHE LaSt SuPPeR

Matthew 26:17-30

On the first day of the Festival of Unleavened Bread – the time when God's children remember their exodus from Egypt – the disciples came to Jesus and asked, "Where would You like us to gather for the Passover meal?"

"Go into the city," Jesus replied, "find a man and tell him, 'Jesus says His time is near. He is going to celebrate the Passover with His disciples at your house.'"

So the disciples did just as Jesus asked.

When evening came, Jesus was relaxing at the table. While they were all eating, He looked up and said, "Listen. I tell you the truth! One of you is about to betray Me!"

"Surely you don't mean me, Lord?" they began to say to each other.

Then Jesus took bread. He thanked God, broke it, then gave it to His disciples and said, "Take this bread and eat it; this is My body."

After that, He took a cup. He thanked God, gave it to the disciples and said, "Drink from this cup, all of you. This is My blood — the blood that has been poured out for the forgiveness of your sins."

Right from the beginning, God had a plan.

The disciples didn't quite understand . . .

But they knew Jesus loved them with all of His heart.

So they ate the bread and drank the wine. Then they sang a song of worship and praise, and went with Him up to the Mount of Olives.

Nane of our mistakes can ever take away God's love.

THE GARDEN OF GETHSEMANE

Matthew 26:36-46

Then Jesus came with His disciples to a beautiful garden. But this was not the beautiful garden Adam and Eve knew so very long ago. No, this garden was called Gethsemane.

"Please, friends, sit with Me here while I go over there and pray," Jesus said to the disciples, "for My heart is broken almost to the point of death."

Then Jesus left them and fell on His face and prayed, "Father, if it is possible, take this cup away from Me! But not as I will. Let Your will be done."

After He had finished praying, Jesus went back to where He left His friends and found them sleeping!

"Friends!" Jesus cried, "couldn't you keep watch with Me for just one hour? Get up! Let us be going! For the one who betrays Me has come!"

Jesus went to the cross to take away your sins.

THE CROSS

Matthew 27:32-56; Luke 23:26-46

"Come down from the cross if You are God's Son!" the crowd shouted.

"Father, forgive them," Jesus replied.

"He saved others. Let Him save Himself!" the religious men spat.

"Father, why have You forsaken Me?" Jesus cried.

"Maybe Elijah will help Him come down!" a bitter man laughed.

"It is finished," Jesus whispered.

The sky turned black. The earth shook. The veil in the temple was torn in two.

"Surely He was the Son of God!" the soldier wept as he fell to his knees.

249

THE
empty tomB

Matthew 28:1-10

The stars came out like they always had.
The sun came up and warmed God's beautiful
world. There was evening and morning, like
the very first day.

Mary and her friend ran to the place where Jesus was buried. The stone was rolled away. They looked inside, but no one was there!

"Do not be afraid!" a voice said – a voice whose appearance was like lightning! The voice had clothes as white as snow!

"I know you are looking for Jesus who was crucified. But Jesus is not here . . . He has risen from the dead just as He said!"

So at last it is finished! God's plan is complete! The path back into the garden is opened once more. And, like a beautiful butterfly spreading its wings for the very first time, we can finally say . . .

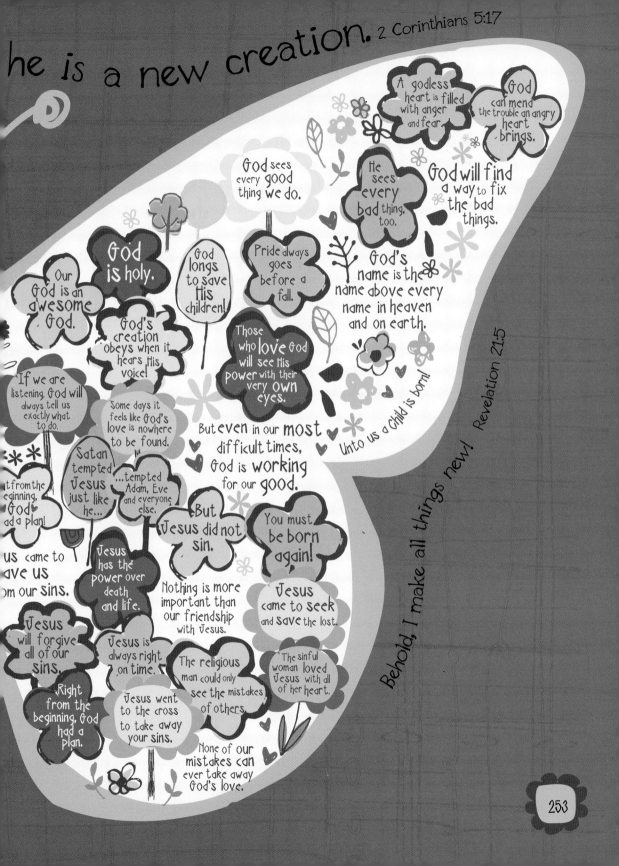

Do you remember the little caterpillar before she became a butterfly? We are all a little bit like her, aren't we? Small, at times unloved, and often not very attractive, but with a lifetime of beauty locked up inside trying to find a way out.

Do the unattractive things take away God's love for us? Of course not! Jesus knows about all of those things. But, just like that little caterpillar, He sees what we can become!

And because He loves us so much, He was willing to step out of heaven, become a man, live a sinless life, and die on the cross to make sure our sins would be washed away so that we can live with Him forever!

Do you want to spread your wings and fly like that little butterfly? All you have to do is ask.

When you say this simple prayer, and believe it with all of your heart, Jesus will make your heart His forever home. And the beautiful masterpiece that has been hidden inside of you will spread its heavenly wings and fly!

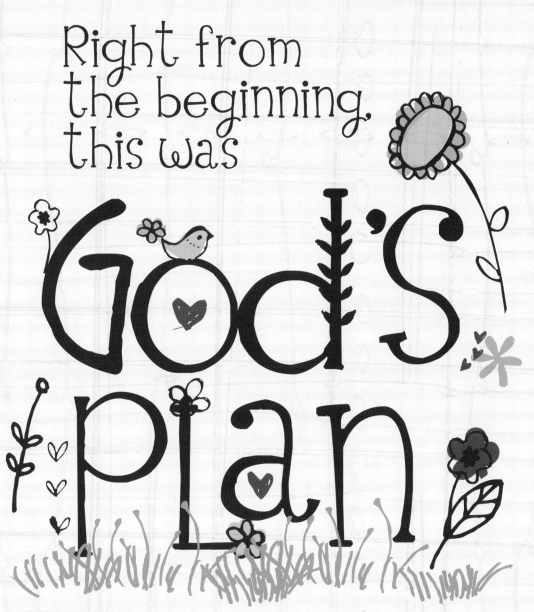

Right from
the beginning,
this was

God's plan

Jesus, here is my heart. Please come and make my heart Your home. I know You died to take my sins away. I want to be like You. Amen.

PHIL A. SMOUSE

Once upon a time, Phil A. Smouse wanted to be a scientist. But scientists don't get wonderful letters and pictures from friends like you. So Phil decided to write stories like this one, and draw and color instead! You can contact him at phil@philsmouse.com or learn more about his other books for children at www.philsmouse.com

AMYLEE WEEKS

Amylee Weeks is a believer, artist, wife and mom. She lives in Iowa with her husband, Ryan, and their two girls. Amylee's life is full, blessedly full. It is a dream come true to create art for the hearts of young believers. You can contact Amylee at amyleeweeks@gmail.com or learn more about her at www.amyleeweeks.com